Our Heavenly Friends
Volume 2

Saint Thérèse of Lisieux

Ever since she was a little girl, Therese wanted to serve God. Even though she was not old enough to join a convent, she wanted to be a servant of God so much that she asked the Pope to let her! Eventually, when she got older and permission was granted, she got very sick. Knowing she was too weak to do great things for God, she made up her mind to do small things with great love for Him. She said, "Without love, even the brilliant things you do count as nothing!" Saint Therese went home to be with God when she was only 24 years old, but through her "little way" she taught us that we can all do great things if we do them in the love of God!

Saint Dominic Savio

Though very young, Dominic loved and obeyed God with all of his heart. One day he stopped a fight by holding up a little crucifix between two boys who were very angry at each other. What great courage and faith he had, but more importantly, Dominic had the great courage to serve God with all his heart each day of his young life. He died at just 15 years of age, but his example of youthful love for God continues to speak to us today.

The Holy Family

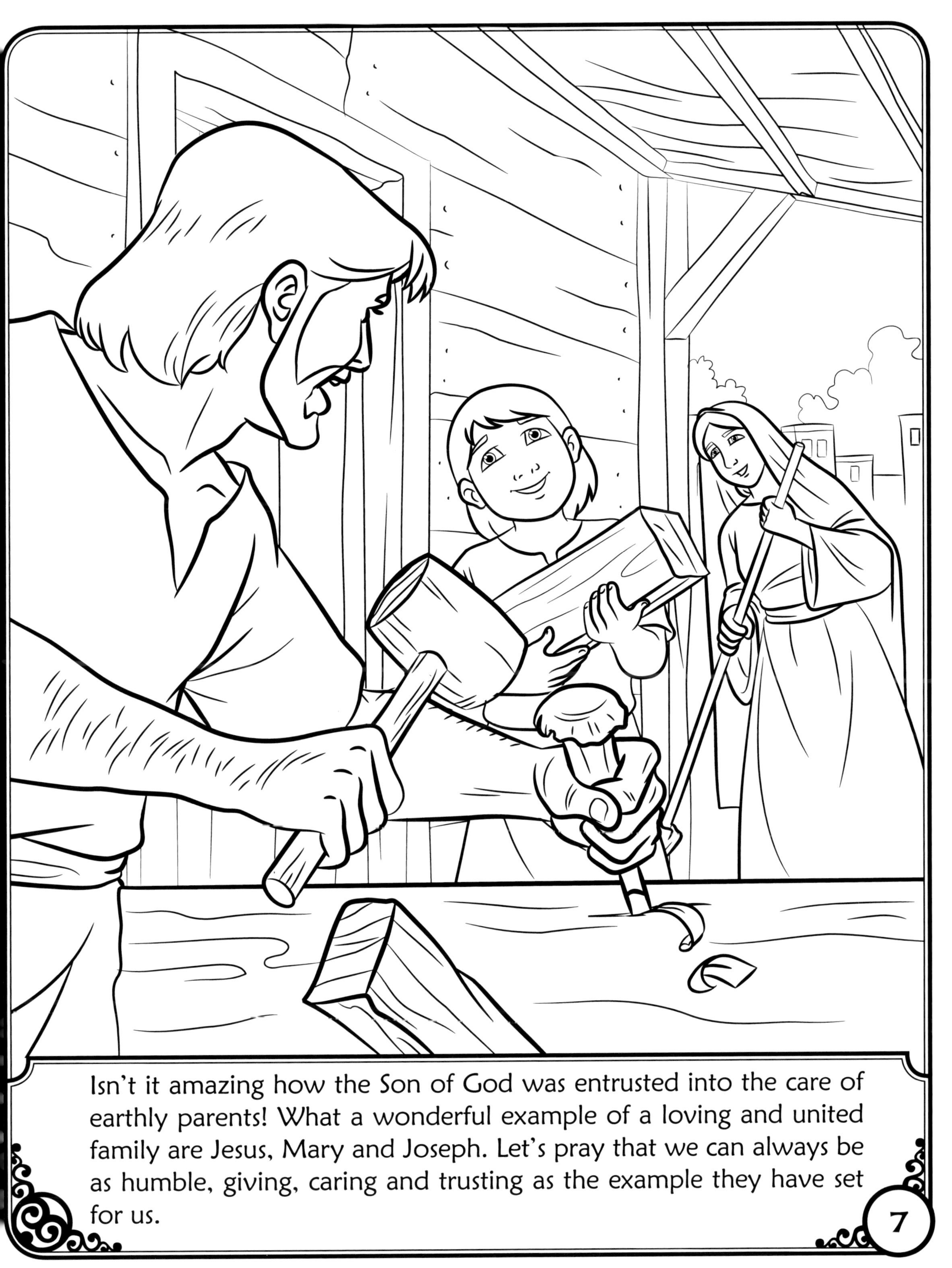

Isn't it amazing how the Son of God was entrusted into the care of earthly parents! What a wonderful example of a loving and united family are Jesus, Mary and Joseph. Let's pray that we can always be as humble, giving, caring and trusting as the example they have set for us.

Saint Rose

Although she was greatly admired for her beauty, Saint Rose wanted nothing more than to serve God as a nun. To the surprise of many, she began by doing all she could to help the poor. Soon she was known more for her devotion to God than for how pretty she was, and her holiness inspired many to come to know God. What an example of helping the poor and needy Saint Rose is for all of us!

Saint Perpetua and Saint Felicity

Twenty-one year-old Perpetua became a Christian just when the Roman Empire declared it to be against the law! The emperor felt that there were too many Christians and he was afraid there would be more. Even though it meant facing death in the arena, Perpetua boldly stood up for her faith. Felicity, her servant, took the same stand. Together they faced the wild beasts that eventually ended their lives, and they died as sister martyrs! They were such an example of faith and courage in the arena that many more people were converted to Christianity! Soon the Roman Empire fell, but the faith that Perpetua and Felicity died for continues to live on.

Saint Stephen

Saint Stephen's name means "crown", and he was the first follower of Jesus to receive the martyr's crown. People loved Stephen, but some of his enemies spread lies that he had said bad things about God. When Stephen spoke to defend himself, he did all he could to show people that Jesus was the Son of God. When he spoke about Jesus, those that heard him said that he looked like an angel. But his enemies did not like him and took him outside the city to kill him. As he died, Stephen prayed, "Lord do not hold this sin against them!"

Saint Patrick

When Patrick was 14 years old, he was captured by a raiding party and taken to Ireland. Forced into slavery, he was put to work tending sheep. It was in this isolated and difficult setting that young Patrick turned to God. Using the lonely hours to pray, Patrick soon began to enjoy a deep relationship with his Creator. Six years later, through a dream, God directed him to freedom. Having escaped and returned to his family, he was surprised by another dream in which the people of Ireland were begging him to return. Convinced God wanted him to share his faith with his former captors, Patrick began to study for the priesthood. Eventually he returned to Ireland to preach the Gospel. Miracles followed, and Patrick's courageous faith soon inspired others to come to God!

Jesus said: "Everyone that shall confess me before men, I will also confess him before my Father who is in heaven."

(Matthew 10:32)

Heavenly Father, the Saints were people who gave of themselves to help others. Help me to be a blessing to those around me by living out my faith. Amen